INTRODUCTION

It's great when young ch[...] phase.

"Why does rain go into [...]

"Why are there white lines in the middle of roads?"

"Why do goats look sad?"

As we grow older, we stop asking so many questions (we start getting asked them instead!). But we don't stop having them. It's just that often life is too busy to get round to thinking about them. Or we're too embarrassed to ask them. Or we're a bit worried about what the answers would be if we faced up to them.

Christianity isn't about having all the answers. But it is about knowing the one who does, God, and listening to what he has to say about life, the world and our future.

So we're really glad you're asking the big questions about life and about Christianity (even bigger than why rain goes into puddles). In this booklet you'll find answers from the Bible to some of the questions people most often ask. You can read them in any order you like.

We hope you find it helpful, thought-provoking, and even exciting.

Now, why *do* goats look sad?!

CONTENTS

HOW CAN WE KNOW GOD EXISTS?

 I can't see him (or her, or it), or test him, or feel him. Why should I believe in God? And if there's no God, then Christianity, and this booklet, are a waste of time!

Two things *point* to God's existence...

CREATION

"Since the creation of the world God's invisible qualities—his eternal power and divine nature—have been clearly seen, being understood from what has been made" (from the Bible book of Romans, chapter 1, verse 20).

Creation is amazing. It's like a wonderful painting, which prompts us to say: "Whoever painted this must be amazing". And no one looks at a painting and assumes the paint just fell like that! So the Bible says God deserves "glory and honour ... for you created all things" (Revelation 4 v 11).

CONSCIENCE

Each of us has a sense that some things are right and some things are wrong—a kind of internal moral code. Where did that come from? Animals don't have a conscience. The Bible says that our "consciences bear witness" (Romans 2 v 15) to there being a God who put the idea of right and wrong in our hearts.

But many people look at the universe and say it's not created by God; many people explain how we got our consciences without referring to God. And people hold strong views on either side!

So how can we know who is right? In the end, the two sides can't *both* be correct! For **proof** that God exists, we need to look at...

CHRIST

Jesus said: "Anyone who has seen me has seen the Father" (John 14 v 9). He claimed that when you look at him, you're looking at God living on earth as a human. Jesus backed up that claim by what he did in history, 2000 years ago. And if Jesus is God, that's unarguable proof that God exists!

So the question we each need to ask ourselves is:

"Who was Jesus Christ?"

You can look into that yourself by reading one of the four historical accounts of his life found in the Bible, named after their authors—Matthew, Mark, Luke and John.

Yes, but...

"You've quoted the Bible there. *Can we trust what the Bible says?*" Have a look at the next question.

"I get that Jesus is important to Christians. *But wasn't he just a great teacher?*" Have a look at page 10.

CAN WE TRUST WHAT THE BIBLE SAYS?

> The Bible was written thousands of years ago... contains some claims that seem far-fetched... was written by people who were really biased... and can seem quite confusing. Why would I read it today in the 21st century, let alone base my life on it?

WHAT JESUS SAID

In the Gospels (the four accounts of Jesus' life in the Bible), Jesus says that:

- the Old Testament (the part written before he was born) is God's words, written by his messengers, or "prophets".

- the New Testament, written by his friends, has been written by God's Spirit, who Jesus promised would "guide [his friends] into all truth" (John 16 v 13).

The Gospels (Matthew, Mark, Luke, John) claim that Jesus is God, living on earth as a human. So if the Gospels are right about Jesus, then we can trust the Bible, because he says it has all been written by God. If the Gospels are trustworthy, the Bible is God's words.

But that's a big "if"! Can we trust the Gospels?

FIVE REASONS WHY WE CAN

1. The Gospels claim to be history—not fairy tales. Luke begins his Gospel by saying he's "carefully investigated everything", by interviewing "those who from the first were eyewitnesses" (Luke 1 v 3, 2).

2. The Gospel claims are backed up by witnesses. Most of the New Testament was written within a generation of Jesus' life. So it would have been easy for people to say: "I was there, and that bit didn't happen". One New Testament writer, Paul, said that after Jesus died and rose back to life, he "appeared to more than five hundred … most of whom are still living" (1 Corinthians 15 v 6). None of them said: "No, this is made up!"

3. **The Gospels we read are authentic.** We have enough very early New Testaments to know that what we read is the same as what was first written 2000 years ago (though it's been translated from Greek to English, of course!)

4. **The Gospels are backed up by historical research.** The more we find out about that era, the more we discover that the Gospels' details check out with what non-Christian writers (such as the Roman, Tacitus; and the Jew, Josephus) wrote.

5. **The Gospel writers suffered for their claims.** Jesus' first followers (including the Gospel writers) were tortured and even killed for what they said. They were willing to die for their claims about Jesus. Why die for something you *know* is a lie because *you* made it up?

Lots of people make their minds up without reading the Bible with an open mind. It's worth reading a Gospel before deciding!

Yes, but...

"Jesus could have got the Bible wrong. *Wasn't he just a great teacher?*" Have a look at the next question.

WASN'T JESUS JUST A GREAT TEACHER?

> I think Jesus is pretty important. He was probably a great man and a wise teacher—maybe even an amazing healer. But it's just too far-fetched to conclude that he was God!

It would be *easiest* for us if Jesus were simply a great teacher. We could learn about life from him; but when we think we know better, we could ignore him.

WHO ARE YOU?

It's only fair to take seriously what Jesus said about himself. Once, Jesus was talking to a group of people who were descended from a man called Abraham who had lived 1800 years before. When they asked if he had seen Abraham, Jesus said: "Before Abraham was born, I AM!" (John 8 v 58).

I AM was God's name for himself, the name he had told people to call him by. Here, Jesus says it's his name. Jesus says he's older than Abraham. So in calling himself I AM, Jesus *claimed to be the eternal God.*

WHAT HE *CAN'T* HAVE BEEN

And that means he can't just have been a great teacher.

Imagine you're back at school, and your favourite maths teacher says "2+2=6". Now he can't be just a good teacher. He's either in charge of the whole of maths, so he can write the rules; or he's making this up to fool you; or he's making a terrible mistake.

Whichever it is, he *can't* be just a great teacher!

It's the same with Jesus—but with higher stakes. Because Jesus claims to be God, he must be one of these:

a liar: deliberately trying to fool us

a lunatic: mistakenly thinking he is God

the Lord: God himself, and so a great teacher, but not just a great teacher.

THE PROOF

While he was living on earth, Jesus deliberately gave some pretty good proofs that his claims about himself were true. He didn't only say he was God the Son, living on earth: he showed it. He healed people with a touch; he controlled the weather with a word; he even stopped a funeral and commanded a corpse: "'Young man, I say to you, get up!' The dead man sat up and began to talk" (Luke 7 v 14-15).

What Jesus did backed up what Jesus said. And if he is God, we can't just ignore him when we disagree with him. If he's God, we need to find out what he's like, and what he thinks of us, and what he wants to say to us.

Yes, but...

"Does it really matter who I think Jesus was? *Surely as long as I'm good, I'll go to heaven anyway?*" Have a look at page 16.

"So Christians believe Jesus is God. *What did he have to say about what the point of life is?*" Have a look at page 26.

HASN'T SCIENCE DISPROVED CHRISTIANITY

> We just don't have any need for "God" anymore. Science explains how the universe works, and what causes things to grow, and what weather to expect. We should only live by what we can prove—not by what some people just believe.

Three helpful points, the *ABC* of this question:

ANSWERS

Christianity and science are giving answers to different questions. Science asks questions like: *What* is this substance? *When* did that thing take place? *How* did that thing happen?

The beginning of the Bible, on the other hand, is much more concerned with the questions: *Who* made this? *Why* did they make it? *Why* are we here? So we shouldn't expect the Bible to offer us answers to What, When and How questions; but we shouldn't look to science to tell us Who made everything, or Why we are here.

BELIEFS

Everyone has beliefs which they can't back up with scientific evidence—even scientists! So some scientists believe that there is no God (without being able to test scientifically that belief). And some scientists believe that there is a God (and they can't test that scientifically, either).

And what people believe affects how they look at the world. One scientist might believe the start of the universe (however and whenever it happened) was caused by God; another might believe it began randomly, because there is no God.

But both views about God are a matter of belief, not scientific evidence.

So, science can't prove Christianity is wrong, nor can it prove it's right. It can't prove or disprove the existence of a God who works through science (like the God of the Bible).

The big question becomes: Does this God of the Bible, who controls his world and usually uses what we call scientific processes to do so, actually exist?

CHRIST

Again, it comes back to Jesus. He once said to a storm on a sea "'Quiet! Be still!' Then the wind died down and it was completely calm" (Mark 4 v 39).

Here's this God who controls everything, including scientific processes. He is in charge of science (he invented it!). The more we discover about how this world works, the more we see how ingenious its designer is.

Yes, but...

"So science doesn't have the last word about everything. *What does Christianity say about the point of life?*" Turn to page 26.

"So God's in charge of the world. *Why does he allow suffering?*" Have a look at the next page.

WHY DOES GOD ALLOW SUFFERING(?)

> Any kind of God worth knowing wouldn't let suffering happen.
> A loving God wouldn't allow wars, diseases and unhappiness. "

Suffering is horrible: and deep down we all feel it's a problem, something that shouldn't happen. That's because it shouldn't! God made this world to be suffering-free: to be "very good" (Genesis 1 v 31), with nothing bad in it. *So why is there suffering now?*

ANSWER

Jesus once said: "out of men's hearts come evil thoughts … murder, adultery, greed, malice, deceit…" (Mark 7 v 21-22). In other words, when people—like you and me—think we know better than God how to live, we cause suffering, to other people and sometimes to ourselves.

Because we reject God and his guidelines for living in his creation, the whole thing is messed up: in Bible-speak, the ground is "cursed", imperfect (Genesis 3 v 17). This world goes wrong—earthquakes, tsunamis, diseases.

God allows suffering because he allows humans, who cause it, to exist. Asking God to stop *suffering* existing in the world is actually asking God to stop *us* existing in the world.

But actually *an answer to this question isn't that helpful.* When we suffer, **what we really need is two things…**

HOPE

God won't allow suffering in his world forever. One day he'll get rid of all suffering and everything that causes suffering: he'll remake the world new, and "there will be no more death or mourning or crying or pain" (Revelation 21 v 4). People will live with him in his perfect presence.

But because *we* reject God and cause suffering, *we* don't deserve to be in that world. That's why God's Son, in his love, came into the world as the man Jesus. He lived perfectly, never causing suffering—but he came, he said, to "suffer many things and ... be killed" (Mark 8 v 31). As Jesus died, *he* took what *we* deserve: separation from his Father God's perfect presence. So he can offer life in God's remade world to anyone who asks for it. Anyone who trusts Jesus can look forward to a guaranteed place there.

HELP

God promises to be with Christians when they suffer: nothing can "separate us from the love of God" (Romans 8 v 39). And he promises to use suffering to help Christians know him better, and become like the people he created us to be. "In all things, God works for the good of those who love him" (Romans 8 v 28).

If there's no God, there's no reason for suffering or hope beyond it. It's just random bad luck. It's meaningless.

On the other hand, if there is a God who loves us, suffering is still horrible—but we can face it with hope, look beyond it to a better life, and trust in the God who promises to help us through it.

Yes, but...

"All this hope is based on what the Bible says. *Can we really trust it?*" Turn to page 8.

DON'T ALL GOOD PEOPLE GO TO HEAVEN?

> I'm a pretty decent, good person. I look after those around me—that's what Jesus told us to do, isn't it? Surely God wouldn't shut someone who is kind, loving and thoughtful out of heaven?!

The Bible doesn't picture heaven as a boring floating-around-on-clouds-strumming-harps kind of life. It points us instead to the renewed world God is one day going to make. It's a real, physical, human existence.

So who will be in this amazing recreated world? Three truths about heaven help us think this question through:

HEAVEN IS *A PERFECT PLACE*

When we talk about "good people", we mean people who aren't perfect, but are more good than bad (no one is perfect!). Heaven isn't good, it's perfect—"nothing impure will ever enter it" (Revelation 21 v 27). It's great to know heaven is a perfect place with nothing less than "100% pure" in it. It would be great to live somewhere better than the best we can imagine or experience in this life!

But heaven's perfect standard means that just being "good" isn't good enough to get in.

That leaves us all with a problem. We can all think of things we've done, said and thought that are less than perfect. And we can't make up for those things: a small black mark on a white shirt makes it less than 100% clean, however white the rest of it is. People like us have no place in heaven.

HEAVEN IS *BEING WITH JESUS*

Jesus said that in heaven he would sit with his friends, eating and drinking (Luke 22 v 29-30). At the centre of heaven is Jesus' throne, and people there will love and serve him (Revelation 22 v 3). So if we're good people but don't want Jesus to be our king, we are saying we don't actually want to be in heaven—we'd rather miss out.

And God's Son Jesus also warned: "If anyone is ashamed of me and my words ... [I] will be ashamed of him when [I] come in [my] Father's glory with the holy angels" (Mark 8 v 38). If we won't let Jesus be king in our lives, he won't want us in heaven—however good or bad we are.

HEAVEN IS *OPEN TO ALL*

No one is good enough to go to a perfect heaven. We've all "sinned"—rejected Jesus. But he "died for sins once for all, the righteous for the unrighteous, to bring you to God" (1 Peter 3 v 18). Jesus died and was separated from God so that imperfect people don't have to experience that beyond death. He died to offer us his status as God's child, with a place in the family home with God—heaven.

So the way to perfect life for ever is open to anyone, "good" or "bad"—if they accept Jesus' death in their place.

Yes, but...

"If knowing Jesus is the only way to heaven... *What about other religions?*" Turn over the page.

"This is all about the future. *What does Christianity have to say about the point of life now?*" Turn to page 26.

WHAT ABOUT OTHER RELIGIONS?

> There are loads of religions in the world. And millions of people sincerely believe in them. So if any religion, like Christianity, says their way is right, and the others are wrong... that's pretty arrogant. In the 21st century, we should be more tolerant. They're all just different paths to heaven.

That sounds great! But if we dig a little deeper, the idea that all religions lead to God means we are suggesting three things that don't really make any sense:

THAT RELIGIOUS PEOPLE DON'T UNDERSTAND THEIR OWN RELIGION

There are major contradictions between the major world religions. Christians believe in one God: Buddhists say there is no God. Muslims believe when you die everyone goes to heaven or hell; Hindus say you are reincarnated.

Committed followers of these religions know that what they believe contradicts what other religions say. Strangely, if we say all religions are basically saying the same thing, we're saying all these religious followers haven't really understood their own beliefs. We're saying we know better about their religion than they do.

THAT WE KNOW BETTER THAN GOD

Ultimately, the only person who knows which path, or paths, through life lead to heaven (or even whether there is a heaven) is God.

And Jesus, having proved he was God's Son through what

he said and did, was crystal clear: "I am the way and the truth and the life. No one comes to the Father except through me" (John 14 v 6).

If we think we can decide for ourselves that all religions lead to God, we're putting ourselves in God's position, and we're telling God we know more about heaven than him.

THAT GOD IS STUPID

"God so loved the world that he gave his one and only Son" (John 3 v 16). The heart of the Christian message is that God sent his Son, Jesus, to die on a cross so he could take our eternal death away and give us a place in eternal life, in heaven.

If there was another way for people to get to heaven, then Jesus didn't need to die. So if there's another religion that leads to God, then God's pretty stupid—he sent his own Son to die when he didn't need to.

This enables us to see why the message of the Bible is good news. It's not that Jesus is one of many options humans can choose from to get to heaven. It's that in Jesus, God has lovingly chosen to make a way, *the* only way, for humans to enter and enjoy eternal life.

Yes, but...

"Maybe Jesus was wrong on this issue. *Wasn't he just a great teacher, who made a mistake?*" Go to page 10.

"I'm not religious at all. *How can we know that God even exists?*" Turn to page 6.

DOESN'T CHRISTIANITY JUST CAUSE CONFLICT

The Crusades... the Middle East... the Inquisition... terrorism. Religions, including Christianity, have always caused arguments, fighting and even death—and they still do today. The world would be a better place if we just got rid of religion.

CHRISTIANS AND CONFLICT

Christians aren't any better than anyone else. So they make mistakes, and sometimes do what they want even if it hurts others—just like everyone else. Tragically, that has sometimes caused conflict, suffering and misery for other people. And when that happens, Christians should be ashamed.

But that doesn't mean Christianity itself is awful. Recently, people have caused conflict at soccer and ice hockey matches. They should be ashamed. But it'd be wrong for us to decide those sports themselves are awful, just because some people mistakenly or even deliberately misuse them.

The truth is that people cause conflict. The mistakes and failures of Christians don't mean Christianity itself is wrong.

CHRIST AND PEACE

In fact, Christ brought peace to the world. He came to end conflict. He taught his followers: "Blessed are the peacemakers" (Matthew 5 v 9). He encouraged people to live at peace with one another, and told his followers to love their enemies.

But he also taught that our biggest conflict is one we don't always notice. We're all at war with our Maker, God. We'd rather he didn't rule us, and we live as though he doesn't. Naturally, we're "alienated from God and ... enemies in your minds" (Colossians 1 v 21).

Jesus was born to bring "on earth peace to men on whom God's favour rests" (Luke 2 v 14). Through Jesus, we can find peace with God and receive eternal perfect life with him, instead of being at war with him and facing eternity without anything good.

So when it comes to conflict with others and conflict with God, what we need is *more* of Christ, not *less*.

CHRIST AND CONFLICT

But... although Jesus came to bring peace, many people still want to be at war with God. So Jesus knew that his coming into the world wouldn't bring peace, "but division" (Luke 12 v 51).

Christ's coming means some people are at peace with God by trusting him, and others are still at war with God.

And that's the only division that will continue, and matter, for all eternity.

Yes, but...

"I think I'm already OK with God—I don't feel at war with him. *Don't all good people go to heaven?*" Go to page 16.

"If Jesus came to bring peace... *Why is there still suffering?*" Turn to page 14.

DON'T CHRISTIANS HAVE TO GO TO CHURCH ?

> I've been to church before. It's boring, useless, judgmental and irrelevant. I'd like to think more about who Jesus is—but if following him means going to church, I'm out!

So, does being a Christian mean going to church?

NOPE...

"To those who believed" in Jesus, "he gave the right to become children of God" (John 1 v 12). It's believing in Jesus, the Son of God, that means someone is a Christian—not going to church.

You could go to church every week and not be a Christian—or never go, and be a Christian.

BUT...

If you're a Christian, why wouldn't you go to church?!

• God has "adopted [people] as his sons through Jesus Christ" (Ephesians 1 v 5). So when Christians meet together—church—it's a family get-together with brothers and sisters who want to share your ups and downs, who you can trust and support.

• "God has arranged" his people like "parts in body" (1 Corinthians 12 v 18). Church members are parts of a body, relying on each other, able to help one another.

• The Bible tells Christians to "not give up meeting together", so they can encourage each other to live Jesus' way (Hebrews 10 v 25). Being part of a church is a way Christ's people obey him.

REMEMBER...

Christians are imperfect people like everyone else. As Jesus put it: "It isn't the healthy who need a doctor, but the sick. I haven't come to call the righteous [people who think they're sorted], but sinners [people who know they're not]" (Mark 2 v 17).

People in church are no better than people who aren't. So we shouldn't demand that church should be perfect, or that churchgoers should never mess up.

HAVING SAID THAT...

Some churches are welcoming communities who try to point people to someone who is perfect—Jesus—in an engaging, relevant way. Others... well, let's be honest, some churches aren't particularly welcoming or relevant, and don't focus on Jesus.

So if you've got negative ideas about church, it's worth finding one which is welcoming and Jesus-centred, and giving it a go before you give up on the whole church idea. To find one near where you live, you could go to: www.christianityexplored.org/find-a-course

Yes, but...

"Being a Christian is just a bit dull. For example: *Why are Christians so negative about sex?*" Look at the next page.

"It's time the church got real. *Surely science has disproved Christianity?*" Turn to page 12.

WHY DON'T CHRISTIANS LIKE SEX(?)

> The world has changed. Everyone's realised sex is great, and that we shouldn't impose rules about it. It's my body, after all. Christians are restrictive killjoys—they just don't seem to like sex. They'd rather say "no" to everything.

The thing is that actually Christians do like sex! Four quick things the Bible says, and Christians believe, about sex:

IT'S GREAT

God invented sex as part of life in this world; and as he looked at it and everything else he'd made, he said it was "very good" (Genesis 1 v 31). God made sex to be great. That's why there's a whole book of the Bible which celebrates love and sex (it's called "Song of Songs").

IT'S CREATED

Because God is the creator of sex, he knows how he made it to be used. The best way to use a computer is to read the maker's manual or online guide and follow what it says, instead of tinkering with it and thinking we know best. And the best way to use sex is to read what God says about it, and follow it.

God says he invented sex to be enjoyed in a loving, lifelong marriage between a man and a woman: "a man will leave his father and mother and be united to his wife, and they will become one flesh" (Genesis 2 v 24)—"one flesh" is Bible-speak for sex. He made this most intimate expression of physical love to be enjoyed in the only totally, unconditionally committed human relationship—marriage.

When we don't follow his guidance, all sorts of things go wrong. Some we can see—STDs, prostitution, children growing up not knowing their father. Some we can't—heartbreak, shattered confidence, self-harm.

IT'S SIGNIFICANT

God made sex to be the most powerful expression of love between two people, where a couple become "one flesh" (Genesis 2 v 24), spiritually superglued together. If we see it as just a physical act that doesn't mean much, we're making less of sex than God intends it for. Christians like sex; so they don't treat it as though it is *nothing*.

IT FINISHES!

No sex lasts forever: and no sex produces a perfect relationship. But Jesus says that anyone who is a friend of his "will live, even though he dies; and whoever lives and believes in me will never die" (John 11 v 25-26). Knowing Jesus is better than, and offers more than, knowing any spouse or sexual partner. So while Christians like sex, they don't treat it as though it is *everything*.

Yes, but...

"I've known great pain in relationships. *Why does God allow suffering?*" Turn to page 14.

"If life isn't ultimately about sex, or relationships, or even marriage... *What is the point of life?*" Turn the page.

WHAT'S THE POINT OF LIFE?

> Sometimes I think I know—other times I know I don't. Most of the time I'm so busy doing life I don't have time to think about it anyway. Maybe there is no point. Maybe there is, and I'm missing out. And I know this is the only life I'll get—so if there is a point, what is it?

ANSWER: TO ENJOY IT!

HOW CAN WE DO THAT?

We can enjoy life if we know we're living the best way we can, and that nothing in the future will stop us living that life. The Bible calls experiencing this satisfaction and security being "blessed": it's like being "a tree planted by streams of water, which yields its fruit in season (satisfaction), and whose leaf does not wither (security)" (Psalm 1 v 3).

Satisfaction and security: if you think about it, that's what we're all chasing after. *And God created each human to enjoy this blessed life...*

BUT NO ONE ACTUALLY HAS THAT LIFE

However hard we work, whoever we grow close to, whatever possessions we own, we'll always know worry, frustration and disappointment in some part of our life. The Bible pictures our normal experience not as being blessed but as being like "chaff, that the wind blows away" (Psalm 1 v 4).

And, however much we might enjoy the present, we know it can't continue into the future: death gets in the way. In

26

fact, the reality of death means ultimately "everything is meaningless" (Ecclesiastes 1 v 2).

Which makes it hard to enjoy anything! Life's kind of pointless.

UNLESS...

Jesus said "I have come that [people] may have life, and have it to the full" (John 10 v 10).

Jesus offers full, blessed life because he's:

- The Saviour: "Whoever ... believes in me will never die" (John 11 v 26). He offers the *security* of knowing we are heading for perfect eternal life with him.

- The Lord: "Now that you know these things, you will be blessed if you do them" (John 13 v 17). As God living on earth Jesus said, and showed, how we were created to live, with him as our ruler. Living his way is the way which will bring us real and lasting *satisfaction*.

So the point of life is to enjoy it—*not by living our own way* and then dying, but by *living with Jesus as our Saviour and as our Lord*. The more we do that, the more we'll find ourselves enjoying life; and the less we'll ask: "What's the point?"!

Yes, but...

"That would mean completely trusting what the Bible says about life. *Can we trust the Bible?*" Turn to page 8.

"You're saying that being a Christian is where life's best. *What do Christians actually believe?*" Turn the page.

WHAT DO CHRISTIANS BELIEVE?

The Christian message is pretty straightforward:

"God saw all that he had made, and it was very good."   Genesis chapter 1 verse 31

God made people to enjoy perfect life in his world, in relationship with him, under his loving rule, for ever.

"All have sinned and fall short of the glory of God."   Romans 3 v 23

We reject God's loving rule—we sin. This means we don't know God and are separated from enjoying perfect life with him, now and in the future.

"The Word was God … The Word became flesh and made his dwelling among us."   John 1 v 1, 14

Jesus Christ lived on earth as a man. He is the "Word"—God's Son, living under his Father's loving rule. He reveals to us what God is like and shows how great life in relationship with God is.

"Christ died for sins once for all, the righteous for the unrighteous, to bring you to God."

1 Peter 3 v 18

Jesus died on a cross. He took the punishment of separation from God that we deserve as sinful ("unrighteous") people, so that he can give us a right relationship with God.

"God has raised this Jesus to life … he has received from the Father the promised Holy Spirit and has poured [him] out." Acts 2 v 32-33

God raised His Son Jesus back to life. He returned to heaven and sent his Spirit into the world, to enable people to know him and live under his loving rule.

"Serve the living and true God, and … wait for his Son from heaven … Jesus, who rescues us from the coming wrath."

1 Thessalonians 1 v 9-10

Christians are people who:

- **turn** away from rejecting God's loving rule, and try to serve him.
- **wait** for his Son to return, to remake and rule the world so that it's perfect again.
- **know** they will not face God's anger at their sin (his "wrath"), because Jesus has rescued them by being punished in their place on the cross.

WHAT NEXT?

We hope this booklet has enabled you to think through some of the big questions about life, death and beyond. But often when you start thinking about questions, you end up with more questions than when you started! And it can be tricky to work out what to do next.

We guess you're thinking one of these things:

"Interesting—but I'm certainly not convinced. I'll go on thinking about it in my own way, at my own pace."

One great way to do that is to use a website aimed at helping people explore the Christian message: *www.christianityexplored.org*
It features more answers to tough questions, and you can also hear from people who decided to become Christians.

"I've realised Jesus might not be who I thought he was. But I don't really know much about him."

The best thing to do is to read one of the four historical accounts of Jesus' life, teaching, death and resurrection in the Bible—the Gospels. Mark and Luke are the shortest. They'll bring you face to face with the real Jesus.

"There are some things I want to ask more about, and discuss. I want to think more about what I believe."

A good local church near you will run a short, informal course for people investigating the claims of Jesus, such as Christianity Explored or Christianity Explained. Or you might like to go along to a good local church service.